Poetry and Time

THE GERMAN LIST

Max Neumann

Poetry and Time

Joachim Sartorius

TRANSLATED BY ALEXANDER BOOTH

Seagull
BOOKS

LONDON NEW YORK CALCUTTA

This publication was supported by a grant from the Goethe-Institut, India.

Seagull Books, 2019

First published in English by Seagull Books, 2019

ISBN 978 0 8574 2 655 0

British Library Cataloguing-in-Publication Data
A catalogue record for this book is available from the British Library

Typeset and designed by Sunandini Banerjee, Seagull Books, Calcutta, India
Printed and bound by Hyam Enterprises, Calcutta, India

MAN FEARS TIME. TIME FEARS THE POEM.

Can poetry free us from time?

They know what it is they do, but do not say it. I would like to apply what sounds like the beginning of a novel by a Catholic author of the penultimate turn-of-the-century, or the manipulation of a familiar film title, to poems. Poems know what it is they do. They name the world, label it, they safekeep experience and preserve feelings with all the rather unique qualities at their disposal. Rilke in his typically grandiloquent way, described it thus in a letter to Witold Hulewicz in 1925: 'our task is to stamp this provisional, perishing earth into ourselves so deeply, so painfully and passionately, that its being may rise again, "invisibly", in us. *We are the bees of the Invisible*' (Edward Snow trans.). Poets, in other words, bring together that which is threatened with being lost. And poems, according to Rilke, allow the buried world to be experienced once again. But only in the rarest of cases do they explain how—and they never say just where it is all supposed to lead.

To begin with: Why do poems do what they do? It has to do with the *movens* of writing. We all die. That much is certain. And it's no real comfort to know that other living creatures—butterflies, for example, or bees—compared to us humans, generally do not live all that long. With most species, time is measured in days or weeks. For our part, we already have a number of decades behind us and, if we're lucky, one, two or maybe even three more to go. There is little to say about the mysteriousness of time and duration. But poems, in their own stubborn way, attempt to do so over and over again. At some point I read, or maybe heard, the sentence—you no doubt as well—that, in the end, art is a rebellion against death. That art desires to 'banish' death. To perform something like a magic trick against the immense, inescapable futility of all our endeavours. If everything is indeed melting away into oblivion, then the poem must do something, must break the chain with which our memory is bound to time.

At this point I'd like to share a secret with you: I wish that the pendulum of a metronome would unmistakably swing alongside this talk, loudly striking the beat—*tak*! *tak*! *tak*! and again: *tak*! *tak*! *tak*! And that these beats, let's say 40 per minute, only pause—but then *every time*—when I read a poem. So, what I'd like to ask you is to please imagine the insistent sound of the metronome—and its interruption by the poem.

To return to the beginning from a slightly different perspective: sadly, the mortality rate of humans lies at 100 per cent. This has been the case for as long as there have been humans; and, though the human being is fully aware of this inevitability as soon as he or she is placed in the cradle, he or she cannot accept it and rebels against it over and over again. Indeed, this impulse has been responsible for a good portion of artistic production over the centuries. The themes of transience, of mortality, are invoked to convey to us the vanity of all human activity or to remind us to enjoy every day to the fullest. Some poets also speak of comfort: they tell us that, in its search for perfection, the poem can make a stand against time. That verse sets all it has against the great pointlessness of human existence.

In a way the poets are right. For the poem is presumptuous. It desires permanence. It wants to interfere with all of this rushing time and bring it a point to where it almost seems to stand still. It wants, if it has a classical form, to endure as a stele above the ashes of a more or less long instant of life. It desires to preserve for perpetuity the acute beauty of the beloved woman, the beloved man. It not only wants to make the world visible, it also wants to save it. The great Yugoslavian poet Vasko Popa, interpreting one of his own poems, said: 'Your place is in the long procession of people of your language who, over the course of centuries, submitted to the same strange work as you: they transformed a little bit of earth and a lot of sky they carried in their hearts into a poem. They did not write poems because they wanted to write poems, but because they did not want to die. They did not want to die, and just as equally did not want to see the people around them die. They transformed the world into a poem in order to save it within a poem.'

I cannot shake the impression that the act of writing poems itself—in other words, the 'strange work' of which Popa speaks—encourages the belief that the poem aims to be both outside-of-time and timeless. For the poets, when they write, are unobserved. To start with, they are the only ones to know about the act of writing at all. An act of writing that is connected to all previous acts of writing, and thus raised to a kind of timelessness in which this ever-repeated, ever-protected act of writing exists. Its tool, its instrument—language—is real and powerful and ageless. In other words, in essence, it is timeless.

Please understand me properly: the spoken language of our everyday is based in time. As is the language of many poems. But the poem, the one I'm referring to, signals that, through its language, it can free itself from reality and thus from linear time. The nature of the poem is irreverence: it has no respect for syntax and rules and conventions and therefore no respect for time's constraints or courses. It can consider the manifestations of time—past, present and future—foolish; it can overlap different times just as easily as it can combine places. Cities from different epochs—Carthage, Alexandria, Byzantium, New York—can be called up in a single poem and fused into one giant imperial city. Poems can work with rapid changes of perspective, with the juxtaposition of the incongruous, and with shifts, including those of space: *here—there—distant—near—directly opposite*. And they work at the elimination of time with such thoroughly refined means that, evaporating the differences between back then and tomorrow, a *perpetuum mobile* can emerge.

In his poem 'Histrion', Ezra Pound takes on the personifications of various epochs:

> No man hath dared to write this thing as yet,
> And yet I know, how that the souls of all men great
> At times pass through us,
> And we are melted into them, and are not
> Save reflexions of their souls.
> Thus am I Dante for a space and am
> One Francois Villon, ballad-lord and thief,
> Or am such holy ones I may not write
> Lest blasphemy be writ against my name;
> This for an instant and the flame is gone.

In a short, timeless moment, Pound becomes many, and these many thread a sort of epiphany through his being, a 'flame' that allows normality and facts to be set alight.

There are other poets in whose texts the radical moment smashes through ephemerality. Here is an excerpt of 'On Sea Urchin Rock' from the—sadly, to us little known—Turkish poet Oktay Rifat:

> that day in the open on sea-urchin rock
> my knees all bloody

a little bream on my harpoon
I skinned it and bit into it
with glee

I bit into the flesh of my people on sea-urchin rock
I bit into the sun the salt nature
all the folk songs of the Anatolian poets
especially my Yunus Emre and my Pir Sultan Abdal

(Ruth Christie and Richard McKane trans)

What comes together here with a hearty bite into a freshly caught bream: light and sea and salt, and the mystics Yunus Emre, dervish and pantheist, and Sufi master and Alevi Pir Sultan Abdal's songs celebrating the endless expanses of Anatolia! My poem in honour of the Arabic poet Abu Nawas, a wine-and-boy-besotted *libertine* of the early Middle Ages in Baghdad, has to do with such timeless moments as well:

Wine wakes the heart for hunting. Hills
and antelope it promises. Drink up, it says,
enjoy, for nothing of remembered life
is left but freshness of the single senses.

A shelled almond's aroma.
Your silver necklace, tinkling.
A green and soft light
in the gardens of Basra.

(Christopher Middleton trans.)

Other poets profess their belief in a poem's durability, its resilience, quite clearly—a belief which—concealed to greater or lesser degree—all poets fundamentally share. A prime example is Gottfried Benn's 'Verse':

25, Jan, 2016

Whenever the godhead, deep and mysterious,

rose up within a being and spoke,

it did so in verses, because in them

the torments of the heart forever broke through;

hearts have long since drifted in the current of broad expanse,

but the strophe roams from mouth to mouth,

it outlives the strife of peoples

and outlasts power and the murdering gangs.

(*Michael Travers trans.*)

This grave piece seeks to impose itself upon us. The choice of words may have to do with the rhyme scheme that Benn set in the original German, or with the fact that the poem was written amid his experience of immer immigration during the years of the Third Reich. It was privately published in 1943 in the series *Twenty-two Poems* and later included in the 1948 collection *Static Poems*. The 'strife of peoples', 'the murdering gangs'—here he is referring to the Second World War and the Nazi regime. The final lines of the poem are similarly unambiguous:

Power goes under in the scum of its deceits,

while a verse helps build the dreams of peoples

and removes them from lowliness:

immortality in word and sound.

(*ibid.*)

The message is clear: only poetry endures. Benn believes in the conjuring power of the poetic word; for him, poems are incantations and, ultimately, timeless.

All of us who regularly read poems come to a point when we ask ourselves why we always return to particular ones. It might have to do with the magical effect of certain metaphors, the musicality, the poem's ability to excite, or simply the sheer bliss of the language—as if the language had waited for this very poem in order to be incarnated, to fulfil its destiny. But it could also be that we always return to certain poems because they give us back a little bit of power over time—because they show no signs of fear, because they suggest strategies of withdrawal, because they ultimately demand a halt to the metronome's beat. Some poems, the more reasonable ones, say to us: We cannot conquer time but we can shape it, or, at the very least, tame it.

You can see what I'm getting at. Time's abolition, duration made even more durable, is the unspoken soul of the poem, its unspoken desire. Perhaps at this point I should explain the title of this piece which to some may seem a little obscure. There is an old Egyptian saying attributed to Cheops, the Egyptian king of the fourth dynasty, who around 2540 BCE had the largest of the three pyramids built near Giza. At the base of this pyramid is written:

MAN FEARS
TIME
TIME FEARS
THE PYRAMID

This is a statement of such wonderful, immense presumptousness: that which has been erected by the hand of man shall, in spite of time, be so powerful and sublime that time will fear it. Poets are presumptuous too. As am I. 'Man fears time. Time fears the poem.'

The great pyramid of Giza has been standing for more than 4,500 years in the desert. Time may have gnawed and eaten away at it, salt bloomed within its grooves, all the tourist buses with their hordes unsettled the base upon which it stands, but it remains, as bewitching and amazing in its grandeur as on the very first day.

That stated, a poem is no pyramid. A poem is made of words and not of hewn stone. It is humble, of small spatial dimensions, pinned down on paper, fragile, forever linked to an individual life and its visible and palpable inadequacies. The poetic subject strives for forms in order to wrest consciousness away from its bind within the unstoppable flow of its span of life. With the world before its eyes, it knows that the finite nature of time can be measured by means of various gauges, whether it has to do with a person, a river or the sky. First and foremost, it is concerned with people: it strives to preserve their perceptions, experiences, discoveries, pleasures, insights. Which is why memory is a keyword of all poetry: the poet is someone who remembers. The poet is someone who writes against forgetting.

As I began to write on my subject, I recalled the following, half-forgotten passage from an early long poem of mine, 'The Table is Getting Cold':

> We talk
> about the time behind us, the time
> we already find great though gone,
> and which now must be collected, freed
> from time.

With this I wanted to encapsulate, as I then understood it, the poet's task: 'To free time past / from out of time.'

At that point, in that poem, when I wrote the word 'time', I felt a disturbing interior echo. Was time life itself? Was it the radiography of all of our lives? Yet didn't this lived time have to be separated from time counted and countable and become, instead, the time of the poem? This game of chess against time's snares may not play the role in contemporary poetry that it once did in the Middle Ages, in the seventeenth century and, later still, in the Romantic period. But today too poems have to do with remembering and taking a stand against forgetting. If they are not plain, beguiling bricolages of language, they are all great or small, shoddy or splendid memory-palaces (in this context of ours I was almost tempted to say: memory-pyramids).

I must admit that I rather like the expression 'memory-palace'. For the fact is that poems are rooms. Novels, regardless of whether they jump here and there and seek their way between *temps perdu, temps recherché* and *temps retrouvé*, in the final analysis are always linear. But poems are rooms spreading out across paper. A painter friend of mine once told me that whenever he perceived a poem, he saw it as a spacious room: one line stretching across the floor, another aslant on the wall to the left and so on. Poems act spatially, not temporally.

We are speaking about the poem against the horizon of time. Innumerable philosophical books have been written on time, but they almost never think of the categories of space and time together and thus have great difficulty expressing anything valid about a poem. In their irrationality and spatiality and freedom, poems can perhaps reveal more about the phenomenon of 'time' than most theoretical works. Even if it may not be immediately obvious. With the opening line of this tiny essay which has already teetered past not just a few chasms, I'd made the point: *They know what it is they do, but do not say it.* For only a few poems clearly state what they are attempting to do with the abolishment of time, why they attempt to transform the acute, the fleeting, into an eternal moment. Shakespeare's sonnets express this in an incomparable way: they speak of nothing but this attempt itself. In his *Die verdächtige Pracht* (Suspicious Splendour), Peter von Matt gets to the heart of the matter:

> He [Shakespeare] speaks about the beauty of the beloved, about the beauty of the rose, about the beauty of the poem. He speaks about beauty as the absolute, as perfection even, and perfection as the goal and possession for which to strive: the great bounty. But then he also speaks immediately about time, plaintively, despairingly, furiously he

speaks about time, which makes of perfection a mere moment. And then he speaks about the poem, his poem, this poem, which fulfils itself in that, within it, he speaks of it: 'this powerful rhyme'. The poem shall safekeep the acute beauty of the beloved woman and the beloved man for all time. It shall wrench them from out of the devouring, sickle-like, sabre-like nature of time. The rose enters the poem, it becomes the poem, and the poem is the rose, but now forever.

And here, as an illustration, are Sonnet 18's final lines (and you'll have noticed that the metronome has paused again for a moment):

> But thy eternal summer shall not fade
> Nor lose possession of that fair thou ow'st;
> Nor shall Death brag thou wander'st in his shade,
> When in eternal lines to time thou grow'st;
>   So long as men can breathe or eyes can see,
>   So long lives this, and this gives life to thee.

The secret motor driving this sonnet (and all sonnets) is an obsession with time and change. Like Donne, Shakespeare lived at the beginning of the early modern era. His generation was the first to experience a true acceleration of time and therewith the growing instability of all things. This becomes a point of departure for an ever-newly-begun meditation on the deterioration of age and transience on the one hand, and the transcendance of passing eternity on the other. So Shakespeare strives for his poetry to not only adhere to the old Horatian topos of *monumentum aere perennius* but also to become a monument and memory archive to outlast time itself. For him, the intensity of love and the experience of perfection *in the poem itself* enter into an alchemical relationship.

'Love's not Time's fool' says Sonnet 116. And more:

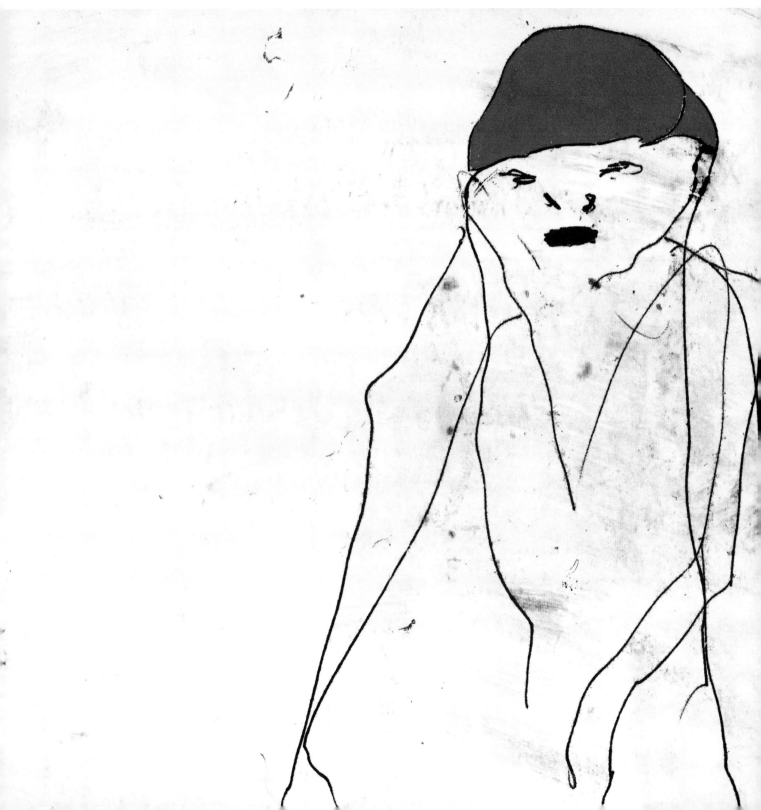

Love alters not with his brief hours and weeks,
But bears it out even to the edge of doom.
If this be error and upon me proved,
I never writ, nor no man ever loved.

This alchemical marriage between love and time will be sealed by the poem. What Shakespeare wants to say is that as his poem will not age, neither will his love. And that is why time fears the poem. He says so again and again, through ever-new attempts, with moving conviction, confidence and pathos. Here is another excerpt, from Sonnet 107:

Now with the drops of this most balmy time
My love looks fresh, and death to me subscribes,
Since spite of him I'll live in this poor rhyme,
While he insults o'er dull and speechless tribes.
And thou in this shalt find thy monument,
When tyrants' crests and tombs of brass are spent.

In all of these sonnets—in addition to the internalized experience of the present— the future time of being remembered and read is anticipated. Manfred Pfister writes that this 'promise of future' has fulfilled itself, for 'with every reading of the sonnets, we are delighted to experience the fulfilment of this promise; indeed, we fulfil it ourselves through the very act of our reading them.'

At this point, in order to clarify, please allow me a brief digression: in Shakespeare, the dualism of renown and being forgotten is always involved, in other words, the old maxim *ars longa, vita brevis*. I am, however, not all that interested in the question of whether a poem secures for itself a place in the memory of those to come. For then the emphasis would be on its social reception, on its reception beyond the death of the poet, and not on the work itself. Czeslaw Milosz called this somewhat dismissively 'one of the biggest clichés of western civilisation'. What matters to me most is whether time can be abolished within the poem itself. In other words: Can the poem allow the passing of time to become meaningless?

Back to the words of Cheops. This saying describes the unusual situation in which time is inferior to its opponent. Shakespeare's sonnets desire to be this kind of opponent too. His verses shall live beyond the grave. Such cases are a wonder—and a comfort that only poetry can give us. I must have sensed something of this comfort when I first began to really read poetry. This was at a French school, and so it was that French poets were the first to speak to me. At the beginning it was Saint-John Perse— who Friedhelm Kemp brought closer to me not only as a translator but in discussions as well—but I soon laid his work to one side for being too hymnlike and ornate. Next came Pierre Jean Jouve and Pierre Emmanuel. In retrospect, I can no longer say what it was exactly that fascinated me so much about these two. In any event, their poems arranged and rearranged my mind like a Rubik's cube with their combinations of sexuality, Catholic fervour, knowledge of psychoanalysis and general doubts about life. Their poetry had a spiritual dimension, they explored metaphysical questions and created the most extraordinary images for love and landscape, decay and resurrection. Back then, reading these poems (and not during Confirmation class), for the first time I perhaps had an idea of transcendence. The spiritual impulse, especially in Jouves' poems, moved through matter itself, and I found this movement to truly eliminate boundaries—the ego no longer so fixed, the order of the material world no longer so 'ordered', even concepts of time beginning to disintegrate. As humans we are made to observe the past from the perspective of the present. The future too. In these poems, however, all was presence.

A little later I discovered the eastern European poets: Vasko Popa, the Hungarian Janos Pilinszky, the Lithuanian Tomas Venclova and the wonderful Poles Czeslaw Milosz, Zbigniew Herbert, Wislawa Szymborska and Ryszard Krynicki. In their poems, the reasons why poetry often accompanies a 'courage of the spirt' unfolded for me in a

28.5.2017   Max Beckmann

8.8.2017

Max Henno

laconic but all the more impressive, manner. 'We did not praise death. Above rails and concrete / we saw angels. Loved. Turned on a lamp / in the library.' So speaks Tomas Venclova of surviving the 'black century' of which he knows only that it is past. As a representative of all of these truly great poets, I would like to quote a younger one now, a Macedonian, Nikola Madzirov, and his 'Outside of Time':

> We are waiting
> for the negatives of our souls
> to emerge from the thin sky.
>
> We are far away from time.
>
> Look, the buildings are asleep already
> on top of the annuals'
> withered seeds,
> the dragons rest their
> tails across the rooftops of
> our houses, then fly away.
>
> For years now we have lived
> in isolated dates,
> in the day-planners of cold pleasures.
>
> Our forefathers long
> statues, they bend their heads down
> onto the shoulders of every passer by,
> but we are outside of time.
> We take eternity and hand it back,
> take it and hand it back . . .

This is an enchanted, magical world of many times which almost seem to be frozen. Like a surreal cabinet by Joseph Cornell. Dragons, statues, sleeping buildings, withered seeds. A theatre-like setting where we, the speakers, the readers, are ripped out of time and must make our way to eternity as if with a prop—we take it and hand it back. As if we were feeling our way around a dream sequence, free from any preoccupation with time.

But, generally speaking, what is the relationship between memory and time? In his Nobel Prize acceptance speech (1980), Milosz identified the 'refusal to remember' as the greatest danger facing our civilization. In his poems, he wants to hold on to as much of the fleeting beauty of the world as he can. Memory is important to him as it guarantees a connection to the past. At a certain point in his essay 'Poetic Tractate', he speaks of 'Memory, larger than my life.' But memory is always selective. Memory is what remains of forgetting, I once wrote. And, as poets are bound to exaggeration, through the power of their words they can have an influence on the passing of time. Essentially, before all else, this has to do with the rather banal difference between 'objective' mechanical time and 'subjectively' felt time: in other words, with the time that is given directly to our consciousness and which is the basic condition of all experience. As an extreme form of the subjective sense of time can the poem shatter time? Talk and dance it to death?

In a good poem there is always a kind of anarchic overflow. When this overflow with its hundredfold convulsions works, time is created anew, and this is dangerous for all that has been passed on and firmly established. The poem engages in the radical individualization of all phenomena, time's too. It steps outside the collective laws of time and establishes its own. As in a children's game, time suddenly has no more rules— it is simply a luminous 'now'. The poem is concerned with this 'now', this currently experienced moment and its weight. And this now-eternity is neither Platonic nor utopian but ecstatic. Emily Dickinson's poems are haunting proofs of that ecstasy. They

4.7.2017

contain the anarchic overflow I just mentioned. Emily Dickinson is a lot of things: a mixture of terror and ecstasy, exuberance and reserve, a visionary who every now and again makes you think of a refined child with her games. A child who wants to remove herself from temporality and for whom time stopped is no utopia but reality and rapture.

Here are the first two stanzas of her famous poem 'Because I could not stop for Death':

> Because I could not stop for Death—
> He kindly stopped for me—
> The Carriage held but just Ourselves—
> And Immortality.
>
> We slowly drove—He knew no haste
> And I had put away
> My labor and my leisure too,
> For His Civility—

And the carriage drives on, with her and death, past the school, the fields of gazing grain, 'the setting sun' which sinks and disappears. It's getting cold:

> The Dews drew quivering and chill—
> For only Gossamer, my Gown—
> My Tippet—only Tulle—

Now, with these things that envelop her but no longer provide any warmth, does she mean her poetry? Eventually the coach stops before a house which seems to be sinking into the ground:

> We paused before a House that seemed
> A Swelling of the Ground—

6.6.2017

The Roof was scarcely visible—
The Cornice—in the Ground—

Since then—'tis Centuries—and yet
Feels shorter than the Day
I first surmised the Horses' Heads
Were toward Eternity—

Within this poem, different times whirl into one another. The poem as presentiment, longer than the centuries, and yet, as far as eternity is concerned, like the blink of an eye. The poem as the highest presence of mind. Finally, as a world of interrelationships, of 'complementaries'—perhaps composed around the same time as Baudelaire was writing— which later emerge again in Proust in such an incomparable way.

In contemporary poetry, if we take even the smallest look around, again and again we find these worlds of shouts, references and 'complementaries'. And one of the subtlest and most luminous world of interrelationships can be found in Inger Christensen's heroic crown of sonnets 'Butterfly Valley: A Requiem'. The setting for these fifteen sonnets is the world of butterflies in Brajchino—a valley in Macedonia the poet interprets as the 'rainbow of the earth' and the place where she shall unfurl an iridescent requiem. Indeed, blossoming nature's wealth of forms, colours and scents are so triumphant that her poems give the lie to the idea of a farewell address. The butterflies swirl up into the warm air like precious coloured dust, like a bouquet of flying flowers that will be kept alive through language. In Sonnet 14, Christensen writes about such butterfly dust:

It's swirled aloft as light in summer's wind,
as ice and fire and mother-of-pearl host,
so all that is when nothing's left behind
remains itself and never will be lost.

As copper, emperor, amanda's blue
it makes earth's butterfly from rainbow hue
in earth's own visionary, dreamlike sphere,
a poem the small tortoiseshell can bear.
I see the dust ascend before my eyes,
skywards they swirl, the planet's butterflies.

(John Irons trans.)

Literary critic Sibylle Cramer has cleverly noted: 'Thanks to her dual-nature of being both phenomena and words, the sonnet-juggler is mortal and immortal at the same time. As an insect, the butterfly awaits its brief moment of happiness. In the realm of letters, however, it is a revenant in the soaring shifts between memory and presence, substance and spirit, life and death.' The sonnet's pure present expands time into space. One line in particular really moved me: 'so all that is when nothing's left behind / remains itself and never will be lost'. The butterfly grows out of its cocoon, for a few days is beauty itself, then dies. And yet it remains within its disappearance, its splendour remains within the poem and there lives on. The transformation of the butterfly thus resembles a complete metamorphosis: from caterpillar to cocoon up through its final stage of life as an imago. You could almost say that the law of existence in Macedonian Brajchino is that it's the valley of metamorphoses. Ovid waves from afar. Nooteboom from a bit closer by.

The end of the second poem from Cees Nooteboom's 'Basho'-cycle echoes the thoughts on disappearance-yet-not-disappearance expressed in Christensen's Sonnet 14. As such, these formal poems stand in relation to one another without their creators knowing a thing about the secret exchange. Here is Nooteboom's poem, 'Basho II':

We know the cheap perils of poetic poetry
And of moonstruck singing. It is embalmed air,

23. Okt. 2016   Max mmmann

Unless you make stones of it that glitter and give pain.

You, old master, cut the stones

With which you can kill a thrush.

You carved from the world an image that bears your name.

Seventeen stones like arrows a school of silenced singers.

See by the water a trace of the poet

On his way to the inmost snow country. See how the water

                    erases it

How the man with the hat reinscribes it

Saving water and footstep, always arresting lost motion,

So that what vanished remains as something that vanished.

(Leonard Nathan and Herlinde Spahr trans)

First of all: Basho is the great master of haiku. 'The seventeen stones' of the poem are the seventeen syllables of which every haiku is made. These syllables become stones, arrows, silent singers. With them, Nooteboom saves 'a trace of the poet' erased by the water. Not only does he save the footsteps, but the water too, and therefore both the earlier, interconnected impressions. This new act of writing, this safeguarding, makes that which has disappeared remain 'as something that vanished'. And Christensen?

so all that is when nothing's left behind

remains itself and never will be lost

In both excerpts a maximum of preservation is implied. Disappearance here is a fulfilled one.

The more I read these two poems, the more they seem, at heart, to speak of a *passing eternity*, indeed to *aim* for a passing eternity—an oxymoron Genet employed when writing about Giacometti's bare and indomitable sculptures.

21. Mai 2015   Max My...

When we add Emily Dickinson's poem to these examples, the circle closes. To her, in the poem's final stanza, all the centuries that have gone by appear:

> shorter than the Day
> I first surmised the Horses' Heads
> Were toward Eternity—

We have to imagine the following situation: the poet is sitting in the coach with Death and looking past the horses' head towards Eternity. But there's another passenger too: Immortality. *Immortality* is the final word of the first stanza; *Eternity* the final word of the last stanza. At the end of the long ride, it seems as if Emily Dickinson has come back to herself and is now ready to step into a different, freer and more timeless space.

And herein there is comfort. Our disquiet at the fact that the world will pass, that beauty lasts but a moment, that love decays, begins to quiet. Clearly the poem can change us and free us from time. It is remarkable that right at the very end of his famous lecture 'Should poetry improve life?' Gottfried Benn came to the following conclusion: 'Poetry improves nothing; rather, it does something more significant: it alters. It has no historical forces of traction, if it is pure art, no therapeutic or pedagogical forces of traction, its effect is other: it abolishes both time and history (. . . .)' Rather tersely and with no further attempt at argument, Benn informs us: *Poetry abolishes time.* Almost as if this were obvious, as if it were quasi-irrefutable.

Sitting down to write this text, I caught myself imagining that, once you've finished reading this, you'll take a few collections of poetry down off your shelves in order to see if any of my claims are true. The very well read among you will consult Marina Tsvetaeva, for you will remember that she wrote a dense, exciting and insightful essay titled 'The Poet and Time'. You will then immediately discover that she departs from a very different perspective than the one covered here. 'Time' for her is not the one which trickles away, the one that comes with a sickle, but the one of concrete, political contemporary events into which a poet, a Soviet one in particular, is born and from which he or she can barely escape. You will find a four-line stanza of hers mixed into a piece of prose, and which she calls 'To Honour Time':

Since I was born *past*
Time! To no purpose and in vain
You resist! Caliph of an hour:
Time! I will pass you by!

(*Mary Jane White trans.*)

Tsvetaeva always found that the 'contemporality of a poet means doomedness to time.' She praises Rilke for being 'neither a command to our time nor a display of it' but 'its counterweight', and has the following to say about Mayakovsky: '[T]his convict of the present day (. . .) overcame (. . .) the poet in himself.' Her conclusion: 'A poet's marriage to his time is a forced marriage. A marriage of which—as of any suffered violence—he is ashamed, and from which he tries to tear loose.' In her essay, this desire, this refusal to recognize time as a 'master' and to break free of its grip is so intense that we feel it tremble through every one of her lines.

Before we come to an end, one more quick trip back to the beginning. Mortality, transience as the *movens* of writing. Time as the poem's enemy. Let us try then—for the sake of sharpening what we have said until now—to turn the tables on this enquiry a little. The fact that our lives will end is not, in the end, regrettable but fortunate. For what would we really do with immortality? Wouldn't the dissolution of sudden, irretrievable happiness reside there? Wouldn't our full range of emotions give way to a monotonous and immeasurable dullness? Immortality doesn't seem even a shade better than mortality. And yet, and yet—all of us want a deferral, are begging for a deferral. Didn't Marie Antoinette on the guillotine ask to be granted just a few seconds more in order to look at the world around her, to see the light play across the blade? Could the writing of poems be a means of begging for just such a deferral?

Cheops' saying is an example of hubris. Shakespeare's sonnets are an example of hubris. No doubt those who are not close to poetry, who do not write poetry themselves, see it this way. The person who questions such a presumptuous, if not arrogant, statement will say: Only in 20,000 years' time will we know if the pyramid is still standing and whether or not Cheops was right. Only in a thousand years' time will we see whether the verse of Shakespeare, of Goethe, of Pound, Christensen and Benn continues to be read. But are these arguments? I call on you to empathize with the poets, to make yourself comfortable with their delightful hubris. For it is obvious and disconcertingly clear: that any poem that does not seek to conquer time is not worth being written.

References

Unless otherwise noted, translations in this piece by the current translator from the author's German versions.

BENN, Gottfried. Translated by Martin Travers. Available at: http:// gottfriedbennpoems.com (last accessed 21 January 2018).

CHRISTENSEN, Inger. 'The Valley of the Butterflies' (John Irons trans.) in *Leviathan Quarterly* 8 (June 2003). Available at: https://johnirons.com/pdfs/sommerfugledalen11.pdf (last accessed 21 January 2018).

DICKINSON, Emily. *The Complete Poems of Emily Dickinson* (Thomas H. Johnson ed.). Boston: Little, Brown and Company, 1960.

GRÄF, Dieter M. (ed.). *Das leuchtende Buch*. Berlin: Insel Verlag, 2005.

NOOTEBOOM, Cees. *The Captain of the Butterflies* (Leonard Nathan and Herlinde Spahr trans). Los Angeles: Sun & Moon Press, 1997.

POPA, Vasko. *Ein Gedicht und sein Autor* (A Poem and its Author). Berlin: LCB, 1967.

RIFAT, Oktay. *Poems of Oktay Rifat* (Ruth Christie and Richard McKane trans). Vancouver: Anvil Press, 2007.

SARTORIUS, Joachim. *Selected Poems* (Richard Dove ed.). Manchester: Carcanet, 2006.

TSVETAEVA, Marina. *Art in the Light of Conscience*: *Eight Essays on Poetry* (Angela Livingstone trans.). Hexham: Bloodaxe Books, 2010.

4. März 2016   Max Immmann

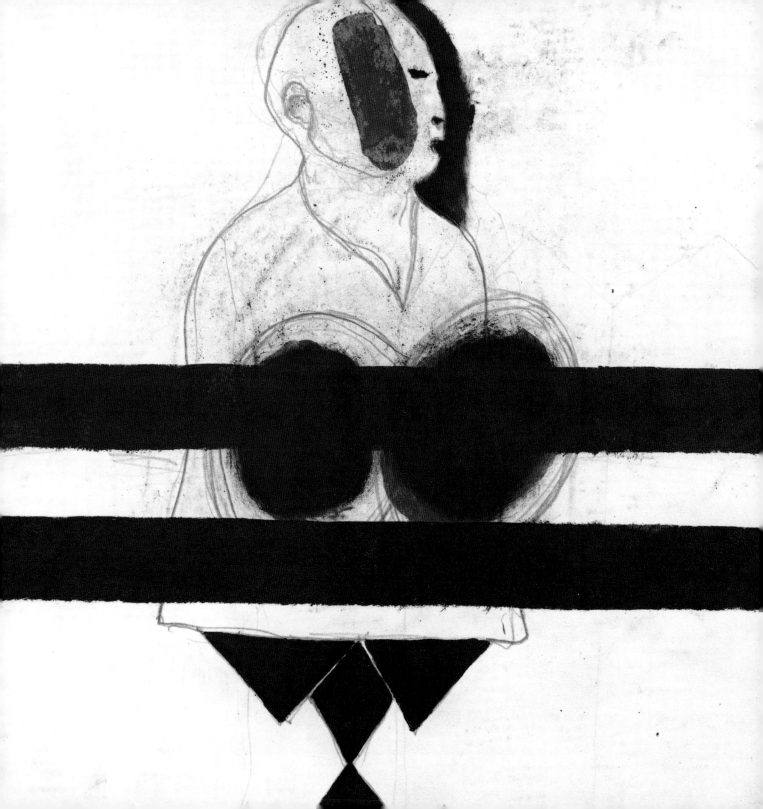

THE TABLE IS GETTING COLD

Regardless of the door we stepped through,
nourishment, leisure,
medicine await us: a place to rest.
Sat at the stone table
in the dignity of countless tiring things.
Too many wasps,
the tablecloth too yellow perhaps
to compliment the knife and the wine.
We enjoy it and ourselves.
Floral-foam for flowers? Three spoons?
No, no books today.
'*Nino è chi si possa gloriare*
altro che nelle fadighe.'
A fierce guessing game begins.
One-and-a-half years ago
we were here. The snow
didn't crack beneath our soles,
there was no snow,
it didn't crunch beneath our steps.
Different colours, of closeness and of wind;
an earlier time of year, of our lives.
The swallows large.

At the beginning, carried to term, small, rosy,
lungs expanding,
stories whispered about your bed.
Their images—of your parents, comics,
films—formed your heart and your
sex. At the beginning, beneath the milk-
dripping rubber tree, alive
in segments, in a language, rolled up
like a hedgehog: from the door, from the windows,
from the castle with its knights, from
Silver Lake, from the courtyards at *Fort Sud*
—from everywhere it came and had
always been, and you grew up
inside it. Now you fish out the old
photo: look at the humble blue door,
the one that once opened to your friends,
familiar,
like the entrance to childhood's tiny
brothel: maids,
a Lampadaire and steaming sheets,
so hot, a blind,
scuffed mirror
on which the blind camel
spins a blind circle round the fountain.
Sweet mint tea. The smell of butchers.

You're still learning
in the puddles of Carthage.
The moon above the horse's forehead
is Baal, the one who devours children
and drives the silver sparrow off
under time's ceaseless rain.
You often dreamt
of leaving. You watched
the sea and the ships
and longed to know where they went,
those ships.
That was the moment you began
to demand pleasure and
solid ground beneath your feet.
So sure of the abundance
and the uncommon
that from then on you'd get to know.
You never once thought about return.

August. The toads are growling by the pool.
The swallows shriller than all the others. We don't like
this month. Evening already thins the light,
grows knives. The little glow-worms
in the bushes will soon be our pale
lamps. We continue to read aloud,
quiet, collected. Someone

22. Juli 2016

has made a fire. The moment we put our books

down, he says, it'll catch us

naked. But we're not afraid of night,

we take pills, like at hospital,

an invocation of its sad nature.

The shadows now are rising everywhere, up from

the smallest fissures, the lowest floors,

from the panes just like the hills

which caressed our retinas all day long,

from our feet, legs propped up,

to those places which are night's outposts

inside our body, which no sun

illuminates. 'The taste of strawberries only

lasts so short a time,' someone says, and we look

at them and think of her breasts

as steadily as of certain names.

'What happens next?' another asks,

a person I love and who's disappointed me.

We comfort him.

We suffered the same thirst.

'What happens next?'

Remembering is such a magnificent part

of life, we console him,

and the heart is fond of the breath.

'There you have your breath,'

out of a single mouth.

Pants on the table, crumpled,
a hint of ice-cream on the fly,
belt in six loops.
You remember
the shoemaker: 'Holes don't cost a thing.'
And Anna: 'I was so sweaty,
I didn't even have to take off my make-up.'
Man's activity: a general kneeling
down before those animal-like places,
dark, simple, so complicated,
breathing in the smells, a true cult.
And the hips were big,
back firm, neck and thighs strong
until trust in their strength splintered.
Indifferent, delicate
shoulders remaining. The gem
leapt out of the ring, the woman caressed
making herself so small
beneath the weight of your love.
At the beginning,
despite all the reversals, all the bitter experiences,
it was the beginning again, was like
a revelation: to see with four eyes,
to find yourself through words and
the illusory world, to enter
into the body of the one you loved.

Later you became the wrinkly little man
she gave a windowed landscape.
Her fingertips mimicked the rain.
The heat broke into yellow and brown
around the motionless hammock.
The inescapable mistakes we
had to make already distant.
We were fond of each other, our limbs at ease,
hearts set right and lighter.

Darker now the welcoming table of stone.
The swallows tremble tiredly
at the windowframe. Their young ones cry:
So bring us something big! Dragonflies and spiders!
We roll the fig cake out of the showy
house and think wistfully about our youth.
Back then we hunted flies we can
no longer catch. Not only that! We talk
about the time behind us, the time
we already find great though gone,
and which now must be collected, freed
from time. But our bones may know:
our poverty, this gesturing
after some immortality or other,
this scribbling, a twisted laugh,
all of life towards the end

a torn and twisted laugh.
To thank us for some milk the cat brings
two dead swallow children. White
sticky slits in masks of down.
Above that the heavy elderberry
with its black fruit.
How long
the sunset is here!
A gust of wind comes and arouses itself
in the sturdy oaks. We bring
our bodies closer to the sounds of night,
delicate black silhouettes on graphite.
The wind blows. A small, dead leaf
clings to his lip.
'What happens next?'
The grappa spread throughout
each and every corner of our mouths.

'*Adunque non schifate mai labore. Io vi*
manderó delle mollicole e del vivande,
como a figliuolo. E voi combattete virilmente.'
And you all: Act like men. What does that
mean? Was there
something like 'the active life'?
In circles no one but you and your friends
perceived?

Indeed, no one knows anything else.
But on the screen,
marked by electron beams,
it's a given: reality
with those black spots
of war and war on an immense map
and its announcement: the cold has grown,
the water frozen, the thinnest of blankets.
A backroom deal.
You leant against your table, only a few things
wanted to follow your demands:
a poem, a friendship,
a commitment, this wheezed text?
'Reality' was something else with those
marionettes from General Motors and Pure Reason,
cortisone and God gone missing,
with its living ones Fanon, Cavafy, Yacine.
In the end everything confused you.
Deserts burned, ships setting sail
sank beneath their load of ashes
(while you slept the entire
time), leant on books,
a whole drama in your skull from here to the Black Sea:
unhomed, journeys pointless,
ice-topped tar in the mornings.

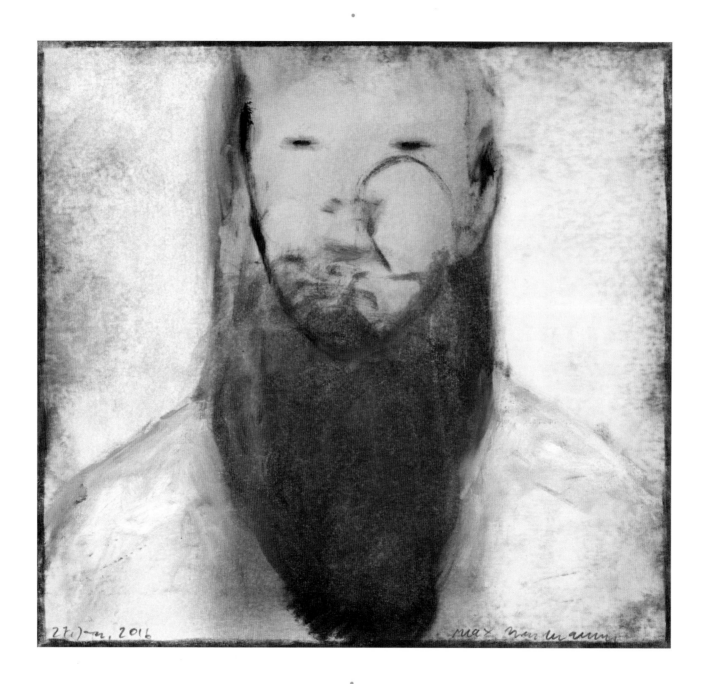

27.)—n, 2016   max Baumann

Beyond that birthdays, memorial days, death days,
traces of breasts in the snow, was there any snow?
A mystery, you can't believe your eyes. But
your very own hair around your very own ears,
to endure
with the length of a life, with a grey glisten,
under a ceiling fresco of Daedalus:
this film, which wasn't spared
or conserved, washed-out, lined with cracks,
like rain on an inky fountain pen,
audio track slightly off,
like your life, lost in the cafe
mirror, the pages, like the bones
of the old man on the white sheet,
dull if a bit blue, glittering at the joints,
layered and cautionary: the flight
leaves shortly. Shortly. Shortly in the night.
Ah, let it go. Let yourself go.
And you wait at the bedside
amid gauze, tomographies and infusions,
newspaper folded across his throat,
you wait, stiff, heavy,
for the years, which move forward,
with nothing but the fear
of a premature end,
for the morning, the bright light.

To the dead '*è terminata la pena ma non
la carità*', for '*l'amore mia vi creà, et
l'amore mia vi conserva.*' Is that how it is?
It's a reaper, and this face falls,
and this hand, and
this wasp wanders through this watch
and this body shall turn to dust.
We refuse to talk.
Nourishment.
The table is getting cold.
Coldhouse.
Coldsleep.
Death.

The cold, old morning
on the railing of the stairs.

12. Sept 2016   Max Lindemann